# MARIE FIELDER: A PORTRAIT

© Fielding Graduate University, 2022
Published in the United States of America.

Fielding University Press is an imprint of Fielding Graduate University. Its objective is to advance the research and scholarship of Fielding faculty, students, alumni and associated scholars around the world, using a variety of publishing platforms. For more information, please contact Fielding University Press, attn. Jean-Pierre Isbouts, 2020 De la Vina Street, Santa Barbara, CA 93105. Email: fup@fielding.edu.
On the web: www.fielding.edu/universitypress.

All rights reserved. No part of this publication may be reproduced or transmitted, in any form by any means, without the prior permission of
Fielding University Press.

Library of Congress Cataloging-in-Publication data
1. Social Sciences – Social Change – Biography of Marie Fielder

# MARIE FIELDER: A PORTRAIT

by
Jenny Johnson-Riley, PhD

Marie Fielder Center for Democracy, Leadership, and Education
Fielding Graduate University

# Dedication

*To Donna Furth*
Whose early work documenting the life of Marie Fielder laid
the groundwork for this monograph.

# Acknowledgements

This monograph would not have been possible without the assistance of many people. My biggest debt of gratitude is owed to Nicola Smith, Marie Fielder's daughter. In addition to participating in two lengthy interviews, Nicola conducted two interviews herself. She provided me with invaluable archival information and patiently answered my many questions. Orlando Taylor, Director of the Marie Fielder Center, conceived of this project and provided the resources to help me complete it. Thanks are also due to Margo Okazawa-Rey, who recommended me for this project. Jeneene Robinson helped digitize many archival materials including the photos contained in the monograph. Gwendolyn Bethea provided last minuting editing assistance, which might more accurately be described as editing magic.

Thanks to Anna DiStefano, Mark Scanlon-Greene, Lenneal Henderson, Sharon Hutchins, Beverly Palley, Judy Kuipers, Richard Mitchell, John Stromberg, and Virgine Thomas-Cotter for sharing their recollections of Marie Fielder. Special thanks are owed to Sharon Hutchins, whose description of Marie Fielder included Fielder's belief that there was "no room for playing small." Anna DiStefano also deserves special recognition for locating several government reports that summarized much of Marie Fielder's work on school desegregation.

As always, I would like to thank my husband, Kyle Riley, for his support and willingness to tolerate my frequent absences while I isolated in my study, researching and writing this monograph.

# Table of Contents

Introduction . . . . . . . . . . . . . . . . . . . . . . . . . . . . . . . . 9

Chapter 1. From Troublemaking Ancestors to Professor of Education . . . . . . . . . . . . . . . . . . . . . . . . . . . . . . . . . 15

Chapter 2. Intergroup Dialogue and Desegregation in California Public Schools . . . . . . . . . . . . . . . . . . . . . . 41

Chapter 3. Increasing Equity in Schools, Municipalities, and Corporate America . . . . . . . . . . . . . . . . . . . . . . . . . . 61

Chapter 4. Mentoring the Next Generation . . . . . . . . . . . 77

Epilogue . . . . . . . . . . . . . . . . . . . . . . . . . . . . . . . . . . 85

The Legacy of Marie Fielder . . . . . . . . . . . . . . . . . . . 85

Endnotes . . . . . . . . . . . . . . . . . . . . . . . . . . . . . . . . . 89

References . . . . . . . . . . . . . . . . . . . . . . . . . . . . . . . 91

About the Author . . . . . . . . . . . . . . . . . . . . . . . . . . 94

Marie Fielder in a portrait from the 1980's (*Courtesy, Nicola Smith*).

# Introduction

I completed the research and writing for this monograph during a time of worldwide upheaval. Shortly after I was asked to work on this project in January 2020, reports of a novel coronavirus, SARS-CoV-2 (COVID-19), emerged from Wuhan, China. The disease spread rapidly through our interconnected global community, triggering government-issued orders requiring people to remain home unless they were engaged in essential errands such as shopping for groceries or seeking healthcare or were considered essential workers. Restaurants, bars, and entertainment venues shuttered, and more privileged segments of the population began working remotely from home. As with many previous global crises, the most vulnerable communities suffered the most. In the United States, racial disparities were particularly pronounced, with one study finding that African American and Latinx communities were more than 1.5 times more likely to contract and be hospitalized with COVID-19 (Mude et al., 2021).

Against the backdrop of the COVID-19 pandemic, the murder of unarmed African Americans, including George Floyd and Breonna Taylor by White law enforcement officers prompted a new wave of nationwide protests in support of the Black Lives Matter movement. Racial tensions in the United States were further inflamed by the conservative media's misguided attempts to conflate the academic framework of critical race theory with any effort to support racial diversity in the public sphere. The White backlash against the falsely manufactured threat of critical race theory led to strained and occasionally violent confrontations between parents and educators.

As these events unfolded, I saw the parallels between the present time and the life of Dr. Marie Fielder. She was born in 1917 on the eve of the last global pandemic, the so-called "Spanish Flu," which was first identified at Camp Funston in Kansas in 1918 (Spinnet, 2017). The reformation of the Ku Klux Klan occurred two short years before her birth. Unlike the Klan of the Reconstruction era south, this new iteration drew members from across the United States. It expanded its White supremacist agenda to include "nativism, racism, religious bigotry, coercive moralism, and economic conservativism" (McVeigh, 1999). Fielder witnessed the world's slide toward authoritarianism in the years leading up to World War II.

Marie Fielder was not a passive observer of the world's struggles. Rather, she played a pivotal role in advocating for racial, gender, and socioeconomic equality during the second half of the twentieth century. Fielder facilitated interracial community dialogues in the aftermath of the Birmingham Church Bombings in 1963 and the assassination of Dr. Martin Luther King Jr. in 1968 to de-escalate violence and promote community healing. She was instrumental in developing the strategies that would ultimately help the Berkeley Unified School District achieve racial desegregation in 1968. Vice President Kamala Harris would later credit Berkeley's desegregation program for enhancing the quality of her elementary education. Marie Fielder also consulted on matters related to school integration and the improvement of race relations in public schools throughout her 60-year career in education.

Fielder directed a training program for the Willowbrook State School in New York, which was then the largest residential treatment program for adults with developmental disabilities, from 1969–1970. At Willowbrook, she worked to improve the damaged racial relationships between supervisors and staff, which were contributing to the mistreatment of patients. She served as an advisor to and spokesperson for the National Organization for Women from 1973–1975. Throughout the 1980s and 1990s, Fielder worked as a diversity, equity, and inclusion consultant for corporations, including Merrill, Lynch, Pierce, Fenner, & Smith; Morton Thiokol; Rockwell International; and Intuit. She was hired to assist the Berkeley, Los Angeles, and New York City Police Departments improve race relations; and she assisted NASA's Office of Equal Opportunity Programs in developing its affirmative action plan. In 1974, she helped found the Fielding Institute (now Fielding Graduate University), which offered graduate-level educational programming for mid-career adults.

All too often, progressive social change is reduced to isolated, landmark events, such as *Brown v. Board of Education* (1954), the March on Washington (1963), and the passage of the Voting Rights Act (1965). To the contrary, historian Dick Cluster (1979) argues that the disconnection of such events from networks that make them possible serves an ideological function that reinforces the inequalities of the status quo and robs current activists of insights that could guide their work. This monograph not only documents the incredible contributions and vision of Marie Fielder, but also makes visible a few of the myriad connections that supported advancements in racial and gender equity in the 20th century. My hope is that it will serve as a timely reminder of philosopher George Santayana's warning that those who do not remember the past are condemned to repeat it, as well as an encouragement that those who study history may find something in it that will help them light the way forward.

Marie Fielder's graduation photo from Manual Arts High School in Los Angeles (*Courtesy, Nicola Smith*).

# CHAPTER 1

# FROM TROUBLEMAKING ANCESTORS TO PROFESSOR OF EDUCATION

In 1999, Marie Fielder was profiled by the magazine *Working Woman* as part of an article on women who worked past the age of retirement. Her profile began with a recollection of her maternal grandfather, an enslaved man who taught himself to read, upside-down, while holding a Bible for the man who enslaved him (Brodo, 1999). Fielder sometimes told the story of how her grandfather learned to read during her own consultancies and professional engagements. This extraordinary feat was included in the opening paragraph of Fielder's obituary, published by the *San Francisco Chronicle* after her death in 2002. As she told *Working Woman*, the story is proof that "I come from a family of troublemakers. It's in the DNA" (Brodo, 1999).

The troublemaking grandfather she referenced was Taylor Redd, who was born into slavery in Virginia. When the family who enslaved him discovered that he could read, they sold him to a plantation in Louisiana. As Fielder's daughter, Nicola Smith, noted, enslaved people who were sold to Louisiana were "sold to the rice fields to die." They generally survived no more than three years after their arrival due to the inhumane conditions that resulted from the cruelty of their enslavers and the harsh conditions of the rice fields, where disease was rampant. However, enroute to Louisiana, Redd was purchased from the slave broker by a family who was traveling to Texas.

In Texas, Redd worked as a laborer, but he developed the skill of woodcarving. In time, he became known for his woodcarving skill, including carving for houses and churches. Fielder recalled that her grandfather also carved flowers on caskets for children who died during the winter months, when no fresh flowers were available. He was beloved by the community because he never charged for his work on children's caskets.

Taylor Redd was permitted to keep the money he earned from his woodcarvings, and when he was freed at the end of the Civil War, he was able to go to Virginia to search for his remaining family. [1] His efforts to locate them were unsuccessful. He returned to Texas where he purchased 300 acres of land near San Antonio with the money he had saved from carving. He donated a portion of his land to establish a church, a cemetery, and a school. In 1871, he married Sarah "Sallie" Scott, who was also a formerly enslaved person. Fielder's mother, Ellee Viola Redd, was born to Taylor and Sallie on December 17, 1895. She was the eleventh of twelve children, and the youngest girl in the family. [2]

Perhaps because of Redd's reading ability, intellectual pursuits were highly valued by the family. Although Sallie herself could not read or count past twenty, all the children were offered the opportunity to pursue a formal education. The older girls went to Mary Allen Seminary, a school for African American girls, and they later taught at the school founded by their father. Ellee was taught by her older sisters, Ida and Virginia, when she attended the school. She went on to attend Samuel Houston College, then a co-educational college for African Americans in Austin, Texas. Ellee concluded her formal education when she graduated with the equivalent of a high school diploma.

Despite the family's relative educational and economic success, they lived in a place and period in history where racial caste dictated the limits of their mobility. The tension between financial success and racial caste is illustrated by a story passed down in the family, involving Marie's mother's experience working as a maid for a white family. Working as a maid was one of the few paid working opportunities for Black women in the early twentieth century. During that period, domestic matters were the exclusive purview of White women. Therefore, when the male head of the White family began giving Ellee orders, she approached the female head of the family. She reportedly told her that Ellee's family owned more land than hers, and if she could not prevent her husband from giving her orders, she would quit. Her employer apologized immediately and promised to remedy the situation. Ellee never again received orders from the male head of household. For Fielder's daughter, Nicola Smith, stories such as these exemplified the cultural peculiarity of the times in which she was born and lived. As she said, "Mother was an inheritor of a tradition in which Black people were able to act outside of the existing parameters of the system, but within strict, unspoken limits."

Ellee married Roy Fielder, Marie's father, when she was 21 years old. Roy was her second husband. Ellee's first husband had two previous marriages that ended when his wives died under questionable circumstances. Community lore suggested that the deaths were related to abuse, although domestic violence was not a term that was used or widely understood at the time. However, the possibility was enough to motivate Ellee's mother to speak to the judge and have the marriage annulled. Marie told her daughter, Nicola, that when her mother married Roy Fielder, "She was seen as having married down" as Roy had not learned to read until he was an adult and owned no property. Nevertheless, Roy was well known in the community and well regarded by Ellee's mother and older siblings, who facilitated the union in a manner Fielder described as akin "to an arranged marriage" (Rosenbaum, 2001).

Roy, ten years Ellee's senior, was a widower. His formal education ended after the third grade, yet Roy harbored a deep desire to improve himself. His first wife had been a schoolteacher, and Fielder suspected that part of her father's attraction to her stemmed from the fact that she could help him improve his reading skills. Roy's first wife died from tuberculosis at the age of 28 after they had one daughter together.

Ellee and Roy married in 1916. Their only child, Marie, was born on March 11, 1917. The Fielders recognized that their hopes for a better life required an environment free from the economic hardship and racial injustice that pervaded Texas in the early 20th century. Therefore, they relocated to Los Angeles in 1921, when Marie was five years old. Roy's daughter from his first marriage joined the family in Los Angeles, but she returned to Texas after three years to reside with her grandparents.

Roy found employment as a custodian at Walt Disney Studios, where he befriended one of the studio's writers. Marie described her father as one of the smartest men she had ever known, and she said that her father thought, "Reading was one of the most exciting things in the world." Also, Fielder recalled that her father thought, "The vote was the most precious thing." He encouraged her to become a poll worker as soon as she was 21 years old. Roy was also a strong supporter of President Franklin Delano Roosevelt, and he was thrilled when Congress passed the Social Security Act of 1935 as part of Roosevelt's New Deal. Unfortunately, as he had predicted, Roy did not live long enough to reap the benefits of Social Security. Ironically, his first Social Security check came a month after he had died, and Ellee returned it to the Social Security Administration, as required legally (Rosenbaum, 2001).

**Early Education**

Early in her life, Marie was recognized by the school administration in her home state of California as an extremely intelligent child. She scored so high on *Lewis Terman's Revision of the Binet-Simon IQ Scale* that the state of California sent a school official to her home to ensure that her family environment was suitable for a child of her intellectual potential. Her high IQ score is noteworthy not only because she later critiqued the socio-economic bias inherent in standardized IQ testing, but she championed theories positing that intelligence was as much created as inherited.

Despite her intellectual potential, Marie did not learn to read until she was eight years old. Her daughter, Nicola Smith, recalled that Marie said as a child she did not make sense of the world through singular units of meaning. Whereas most people see a sentence composed of individual words strung together to form a thought, Marie was a holistic thinker who looked to the meaning of an entire story or whole book to make sense of the smaller parts, that is, the meaning of the words as whole contained within a sentence. Therefore, in her early years, this thought process and understanding of the world thwarted her attempts to read. She finally learned to read with the help of a devoted teacher who took the young Marie on her lap and showed her how the letters in the book added up to words, and how, when the words were spoken aloud, they created the speech she heard every day. As Marie later noted, this realization was a profound experience for her, and it shaped the rest of her life. She remembered throughout her life the smell of the perfume and the gentle way in which the teacher held her on her lap as she taught her to read. In fact, she credited her determination to devote her life to education to the assistance of that one beloved teacher who taught her to read and enabled her to have a successful life.

Once Marie experienced the epiphany that helped her learn to read, her educational journey was underway. Unlike racially segregated schools in the south, public schools in Los Angeles were officially integrated. Marie recalled, however, that the schools she attended were affected by de facto segregation, with the student bodies gradually becoming more and more African American as she progressed through her elementary and secondary education. Fielder attributed the shift in her school's racial demographics to the tendency of White families to leave the neighborhood as more African American families moved into it.

One of Marie's early academic achievements was gaining admission to the high-ranking Manual Arts High School in Los Angeles, where she achieved high academic marks. One of her teachers encouraged her to attend the University of

Chapter 1: From Troublemaking Ancestors to Professor of Education

Marie Fielder in the 1930's (*Courtesy, Nicola Smith*).

Southern California (USC) and offered to help her obtain a fellowship. As she later said to her daughter, Marie used the dictionary to learn what a "fellowship" entailed. According to the dictionary definition, a fellowship covered the cost of tuition but not room and board. Had she accepted the fellowship, she would have enrolled at USC during the height of the Great Depression. Her family was already struggling to make ends meet. Her father had lost his job, and the family was in the process of losing the home they had been able to purchase after establishing themselves in Los Angeles. Marie knew she could not survive on the fellowship alone. She did not confide her family's financial difficulties to the teacher who had offered to help her with the fellowship, rather, she began avoiding her. Marie later told her daughter of the shame and embarrassment she felt whenever she encountered the teacher, who looked at her with a combination of puzzlement and hurt.

During her adolescent years, Marie went to visit her grandmother, Sallie Redd, in Texas, as it was her mother, Ellee's, wish that Marie become acquainted with her grandmother and her Texas family and experience the rural life that her family had left behind. On a visit to her grandmother's home in Texas, Marie caught the eye of one of the leading White families in town due to an unfortunate incident involving White boys. At that time, African American women did have the option of refusing White men's sexual advances, and Marie was no exception. Marie's grandmother, however, held considerable sway in the community. She was warned that several young White men planned to visit her home that evening. They very likely had intentions of "sporting" with Marie, the decried, but accepted, practice of sexually assaulting attractive women of color at the time. Upon hearing this news, Marie's grandmother arranged for her to take the train back to California that afternoon. The young men arrived at her grandmother's home and demanded that Marie be sent out to them. Her grandmother, Sallie Redd, came to the door and told them that Marie had gone back to California and would not be returning. Her grandmother felt that her reason for sending Marie home was self-explanatory. However, for Marie, this explanation was insufficient and required further examination. This experience influenced Marie's sense of vulnerability as an African American woman.

In the following years, Marie graduated from Manual Arts High School. During her late adolescence, she contracted tuberculosis. The indicated public health intervention for tuberculosis at the time was isolation in a public sanatorium. Marie's best friend, Marie Moss, had been diagnosed with tuberculosis before Marie and was confined to a sanatorium. While visiting her friend at the sanatorium, she began to fear that she would die if she too were sent there. Marie then ran from the public health authorities. Moss did eventually die of the disease. According to Marie's daughter, Nicola, "This too was a defining moment and a defining situation for Mother. At an early age, she understood her survival could depend on her coming up with her own way of doing things."

## Undergraduate Education

As the tuberculosis cases that were prevalent in Los Angeles during the 1930s subsided, Marie enrolled at Los Angeles City College and later transferred to USC. She later recalled a statistics course that she had taken with a Dr. Crawford, who inspired her love of statistics. During her time at USC, she also earned second place in an all-city archery tournament, a skill which she had acquired from a mandatory gym class. Yet, when reflecting on her time in college, Fielder said, that when she entered the university, "The white world was still a great mystery to me. It was as though white people were always standing on their heads, and I couldn't work them out." She recalled a specific incident that illustrated this particular perspective. One day after class, one of her favorite professors told her that she needed to see the dean. The professor provided her with the date and time of her appointment. Fielder said that when she arrived at the dean's office, she found herself in a meeting of the Dean's Council and under the scrutiny of 12 White men. She introduced herself, and the dean asked, "How can you be so smart, and not know anything?" Fielder was confused and tried to understand what he meant.

After a few unsatisfying exchanges, she said, "Well, I walked past the statue of Tommy Trojan [the mascot of USC] on my way to the administration building this afternoon. If you were to ask me who the sculptor was, I would say Michelangelo."

The dean hit the ceiling, roaring, "Why don't you say you don't know?"

A young professor, also a member of the Dean's Council, chimed in, "She's trying to communicate with you. She's trying to tell you she does not understand the question that you're asking. She's trying to dialogue with you."

Fielder sat in silence while the White men talked around her. As she later said, she sat there sweating for the next 20 minutes while members of the Dean's Council fought over whether her response was an intelligent or unintelligent one. Finally, the dean turned to her and said she could leave.

A few days later, when her professor asked how her meeting with the dean had gone, Marie, still puzzled by the incident, responded, "Hell, if I know!"

Her professor explained that the meeting was due to Fielder's scoring in the upper third of the 99$^{th}$ percentile on an IQ test recently administered to all the students at USC. The dean was so shocked and disbelieving that an African American woman could score so highly that he wanted to meet with her. When asked how she felt about having achieved that score, Fielder recalled, "Well, I didn't get a big head because my girlfriend placed in the upper quarter of the 99$^{th}$ percentile!" (Rosenbaum, 2001).

While at USC, Fielder began giving talks at meetings held by various women's clubs that were connected to the university. The clubs were comprised of middle- and upper-class women who were, most notably, Jewish. This fact became important to her later career development. These clubs often featured speakers who had unique experiences or insights into contemporary phenomena. As an African American woman attending college in the early 1940s, Fielder became a popular guest speaker at these events, commenting on books or addressing a contemporary issue. As a result of these engagements, Fielder became close with several of these women who found her ability and perspective intriguing. Many of them mentored and supported her career as she completed her undergraduate education. Her mentors wanted her to continue her education, and even if she married, as she did in 1942, they wanted her to attend graduate school. Indeed, Fielder later said her involvement with these women, the clubs, and the speaker boards which listed her served as a "finishing school" for her. She added that those interactions set her course and defined her style throughout her life.

## Marriage and Family

The combination of Marie's presence, her academic knowledge, her common sense, her sense of humor, and her good looks (her daughter's friend, Donna Furth, said she resembled Lena Horne) also influenced her personal life. Marie met Frank Smith II during her final years at USC. He had graduated some years earlier and was enrolled in the doctoral program in history. They married in 1942, the same year she graduated from USC. Before he completed his doctoral studies and shortly after they married, he became an Army Warrant Officer and served in Europe. In 1943, during his time in the Army, Marie gave birth to their son, Frank Smith III. She began working as a teacher at Jefferson High School in the Los Angeles Unified School District. She was teaching at Jefferson when Frank returned home from the war in 1945. During their time apart, both had changed. Frank dropped his academic studies and joined the Pepsi-Cola Corporation. Marie had grown personally and professionally. She was developing a career in education and was a sought-after women's speaker. Soon the marriage between Marie and Frank began to fail. Shortly before they separated, Fielder became pregnant for a second time. Her mentors, who regarded her as a protégé, advised her that she did not have to have a second baby. They offered to help her terminate the pregnancy if she wished, advising her that it would be difficult to re-marry if she had two children. Faced with the decision of whether to continue the pregnancy, Fielder also sought the counsel of her father. Her father observed that it was good to have a choice, and he and her mother would love her regardless of her decision.

He added that sometimes the very child you "lose" is the one who ends up making the greatest difference to you. Fielder continued with the pregnancy. Yet, as she said afterward, it was a troubled time for her. Her family had never known divorce. It was unknown and incomprehensible to her family and close community at the time. Her daughter, Nicola Ellee Smith, was born in 1946, just before Marie's divorce from Frank was finalized.

**Early Teaching Career and Graduate Education**
While working as a teacher at Jefferson High School, where she taught social science, English, public speaking, and bookkeeping, Marie earned her master's degree at USC. She graduated in 1947. In 1950, she left for Chicago to begin her doctoral studies at the University of Chicago. Prior to her departure, two of her mentors from USC, Dr. Jane Hood and Dr. Bloomberg, called the dean of the School of Education and told him that they were sending him their baby, and they wanted him to take good care of her. [3] She recalled, "I arrived in Chicago with a baby under each arm, and a brief case in between my teeth." She was able to undertake her studies because she was promised a Sigmund Livingston Fellowship. The Livingston Fellowship typically provided recipients with $5,000 to cover their cost-of-living expenses while recipients pursued their degrees. When she was to begin her program, upon the grant administrators discovering that she was a woman, Marie was informed that her award had been reduced to $2,500. Her status as a single parent with two small children was not seen as a reason for her to receive the full award.

However, while at the University of Chicago, Fielder

became a part of President Robert Maynard Hutchins' social circle. Hutchins, the "University of Chicago's Boy President," was installed as the fifth president of the University in 1929, and throughout his tenure, he instituted controversial policies rooted in his questioning of the purposes of higher education and the role of the university in the community (McNeill, 1991). Although Fielder faced many challenges as an African American woman, when the subject of her career would arise, she would remind her audiences, including students and family, that she had benefited from the support of many mentors. She would stress the importance of strategic relationships for developing professional opportunities and a sense of self as a professional. Just as she had formed personal relationships with the women who had invited her to speak at their clubs and associations, Fielder had developed close relationships with her graduate school professors. Smith remembered her mother recalling that she navigated those inner circles by remaining primarily in an observational capacity, never becoming the lightning rod during these interactions. As a newcomer and an outsider, such a stance allowed her to find her footing and establish herself with the unwritten rules of the group before taking any definitive action. Smith said, "Mother never fully understood why I didn't know the trailblazers in my areas of interest, because for her that was axiomatic for the professional." To illustrate this point, Smith recalled a conversation with her mother in the early 1980s regarding her love of a *Star Wars* book and movie before it became a franchise. She said her mother was seriously disappointed, given the strength of her daughter's interest, that she had not pursued a personal friendship with George Lucas. Fielder told Smith that since Lucas lived nearby in Marin County, she should contact him to share her ideas about future movie installments.

The social and professional networks that Fielder created throughout her life played a crucial role in her ability to advocate for policies promoting racial and gender equity within schools, businesses, and the Civil Rights Movement, as did the intellectual training she received during her doctoral education. While still completing her doctoral studies, Fielder identified her participation in the study of IQ testing at the University of Chicago as one of the pivotal periods in her life. She listed her professors, Allison Davis and Robert Havighurst, as two particularly influential figures.

Echoes of each of these scholars can be found throughout Fielder's career, and Fielder said that her involvement with their research, "gave me a different picture of myself as a thinker, a scholar, a theorist, a practitioner, and an internationalist." Allison Davis was the first full-time African American professor at the University of Chicago. In 1945, he directed the first empirical study to measure racial and cultural bias in IQ testing under the auspices of the Committee on Human Development. His pioneering research challenged contemporary educational theories and found that standardized tests favored students from middle-class backgrounds and underestimated the intellectual capabilities of students of lower socioeconomic status (Hillis, 1995).

Robert Havighurst collaborated with Davis on his studies of cultural bias in IQ testing, and he was a part of Davis' efforts to expand the scope of intercultural education. He is perhaps most well-known for his developmental task theory, and he was an early proponent of lifespan approaches to human development (Manning, 2010).

Fielder was quick to apply what she learned at the University of Chicago in educational settings back in California. In 1950, shortly after she began her doctoral studies, Fielder gave a talk in Pasadena criticizing the cultural bias inherent in standardized IQ Testing. Fielder argued that standardized IQ tests place too much emphasis on vocabulary and reading ability at the expense of what she termed "common cultural knowledge." She said,

> "A child will understand problems presented in terms of his environment. The same child who makes high marks in tests based in abstracts are inclined to rate far below other pupils in carrying out actual projects based on such abstracts. Test-makers are arbitrarily defining intelligence in terms of their own narrow points of view."

Her journey to improve the quality of public education for all schools was underway.

Fielder was a doctoral student, but she was also a single mother raising two young children. While other mothers were volunteering their time as Girl Scout troop leaders or chauffeuring their children to various activities, Fielder's children received an early education in independence. Smith said, "Our growing up was never Mother's primary reason for being and that was evident to me as a child." She remembered an incident that occurred when she was around four years old, and her brother was seven. Fielder brought her children to a store and left them under a large clock in the toy department. She told them to amuse themselves but not to be a nuisance. They were to meet her back underneath the clock in one hour.

Smith recalled being very frightened, but she recalled that her brother felt pride in the responsibility he was given.

Fielder's child rearing methods drew criticism from her friends and colleagues, many of whom were well-respected and well-published scholars. They warned Fielder that her children would be damaged by her belief that children could be fully functional people at a very early age. According to Smith, "She gave you every support and security, but she did ask a lot of you. She asked you to think and figure things out for yourself. She also expected you to give a good account of your actions." Although Smith noted that both she and her brother "had their own checkered histories with education," they both lived up to the legacy of their great grandfather and the family members who followed him by earning multiple postgraduate degrees at the University of Chicago and Harvard.

Smith provided another anecdote that illustrates the overlap between Fielder's parenting style and her teaching methods. Fielder had a distant cousin with a developmentally delayed three-year-old child. Her cousin asked her to babysit the child while she took care of a few errands. Fielder agreed, and the child's mother told her that the child was unable to speak. It was a hot and humid summer day in Los Angeles, and shortly after his mother left, the child started making a lot of noise. Fielder asked him if he was thirsty. He made more noise in response. She got him some water, and as she was giving it to him, she repeated the word "water." She gave him five sips before taking the glass back into the kitchen. The child was still thirsty, but she would not allow him to satiate himself until he said the word. She repeated the same technique with the word "lights," turning them off and on until he was able to say "lights." When the boy's mother returned home, Fielder told her that, although her son was somewhat developmentally delayed, he was capable of more than she thought. His mother insisted that her son was unable to speak until Fielder demonstrated otherwise. Fielder held an abiding belief that people may have limitations, but if such limitations were augmented with expectations, navigating the world could be possible.

Having completed her doctoral research in 1952, Fielder returned to her former teaching position at Jefferson High School. Yet, she struggled to finish writing her dissertation. Smith noted that her mother had a "genius level IQ and could effortlessly maintain an incredible number of initiatives at the same time, but she also had some notable deficiencies in her professional skillset," which she never allowed to define her. Chief among those deficiencies was her lack of writing ability. Therefore, Fielder published relatively little during her lifetime. Her work tended to be action-oriented, and the majority of her writings consisted of proposals and reports. Despite these challenges, Fielder completed her dissertation, titled *The Social System of the School – A Study of School Culture as Lived and Reported by Students*. She was awarded a PhD in Education in 1960.

## Relocation to the Bay Area

In the late 1950s, prior to the completion of her Ph.D., Marie Fielder began searching for employment in the San Francisco Bay Area. Her daughter, Nicola Smith, recalled that her parents' divorce caused her mother to look for a fresh start outside of Los Angeles, which she felt was the domain of her ex-husband. Fielder's first job in the Bay Area was at San Francisco State College (now San Francisco State University).

## Chapter 1: From Troublemaking Ancestors to Professor of Education

She taught at San Francisco State for two years before she obtained a job at the University of California, Berkeley.

Fielder bought a house in Berkeley in 1959. Although her home was not specifically targeted by a racial covenant prohibiting its sale to African Americans, a White realtor had advised Mrs. Dyer-Bennett, an earlier, White, owner of Fielder's home, that her home would not be sold to any "undesirables," meaning people of color. To protest the realtor's remarks, Mrs. Dyer-Bennett found an African American couple who were interested in purchasing her home, and she sold it to them at a steep discount. Smith recalled that the story of Mrs. Dyer-Bennett was just one example that her mother drew upon when she insisted that some of the heroes of African American uplift were White.

Smith said before her mother purchased their Berkeley home, she attempted to purchase a house in San Francisco. Her offer was rejected, and the owners later sold their home to a White couple for 20 percent below Fielder's offer. Smith observed, "One could nourish some rightful resentment about that experience, but Mother didn't have time for much resentment." When Fielder sought financing for the Berkeley house, she completed all the required paperwork without meeting the loan officer in person. The loan officer knew she was a professor at San Francisco State College, and he approved her loan for what was the then going rate of 3 percent. Fielder was pleased with how smoothly the process had gone. She signed the paperwork and mailed it to the mortgage company. A few days later, she was in the neighborhood of the mortgage company, and she stopped by to thank the loan officer because the process had been so efficient. He asked, "You're Dr. Marie Fielder?" She said she was, and she wanted to thank him. The loan officer canceled her loan, and she later secured a loan at a rate of 6 percent.

Smith recalled that her mother thought that experience "was just the funniest thing." Fielder told her daughter that was the price of being Black, adding, "It's the price of being Black that you've just got to go on and face. You also have some of the benefits of being Black." Smith responded, "Tell me again about those benefits." Fielder refused to be embittered by the experience and took them as a matter of course. Her daughter believes that Fielder's ability to take such hurtful experiences in stride was a part of what allowed her to create such a diverse network. She said, "Mother's network extended from the people who run the machinery of society right down to the people who are being mishandled that machinery."

## Creating Intelligence Conference

As Smith reflected on her mother's work during the early 1960s, one of the projects that stood out most clearly to her was the Creating Intelligence Conference. The conference drew on research by Getzels and Jackson (1962). Their findings challenged the prevailing theory of human intelligence, which posited that intelligence was innate. Getzels and Jackson suggested that intelligence could be enhanced given the appropriate learning environment, and Fielder was intrigued by the opportunities their findings could create for students who had been historically regarded as unable to attain high levels of academic achievement.

To attract attention to the conference, Fielder called on her already extensive professional network, securing the participation of a psychologist and a medical doctor, both of whom taught at Stanford. Most mind-boggling to Smith was her mother's decision to invite actor Ivan Dixon, the African American star of the popular television show *Hogan's Heroes*, to attend the conference. Fielder had heard Dixon was involved in civil rights work, and she did not let the fact that she had never met him stop her from contacting him. Smith recalled thinking her mother "was certifiable" for inviting Dixon, but he came to the conference. Smith compared his attendance to Lady Gaga promoting an academic conference, but for Fielder, her ability to involve Dixon in the Creating Intelligence Conference was unremarkable and simply a matter of course.

The conference proceedings concluded that intelligence was not fixed. Rather, they posited that intelligence was conceivably a range, and circumstances would dictate the intellectual ability a person could achieve within that range. Furthermore, the range may not be an accurate predictor of a person's intelligence across domains. Smith remembered that the conclusions of the Creating Intelligence Conference were 30 years ahead of their time. Moreover, the conference was successful in attracting a large audience to attend an event that focused largely on scholarly ideas. Smith recalled that similar conferences of the day were fortunate if they could draw 50 attendees who each paid one dollar for admission. Five hundred people attended Fielder's conference, and each paid five dollars for admission. Fielder had to turn people away and schedule a second day for the conference to meet the demand.

### Activism During the 1960s

Throughout the 1960s, Marie Fielder was involved in a variety of progressive social movements, and her participation was often sought in forums designed to advise changes in public policy. Governor Jerry Brown appointed Fielder to the Commission on the Status of Women in the early 1960s. Smith worked with her mother and supported her efforts. She recalled that her mother mobilized the entire household to participate in her activism, much to the chagrin of Smith's older brother. Fielder also served as a member of an informal network of academics in the Bay Area who advised local leaders on issues pertaining to civil rights. Although she had left San Francisco State College by the time the student strike began in November 1968, she played a role in advising both the students and the college administration, including San Francisco State College President S.I. Hayakawa.

Fielder's activism during the 1960s proved to be the most difficult period in her life on which to obtain information. Nearly every person interviewed for this project was aware of Fielder's involvement in the Civil Rights Movement, but few had information on the specifics of her involvement. Lenneal Henderson was the one exception. Henderson met Marie Fielder when he was a student at Lowell High School in San Francisco. Henderson, who was one of only a few African American students at Lowell, was delighted when Marie Fielder was featured as a guest speaker at a school assembly. He recalled that after the assembly, Fielder approached him, put her arm in his arm, and said, "Come with me, young man. You're not doing anything important." He admitted that she was right. She asked many questions about his plans for the future and wanted to know how he intended to contribute to the community. Henderson said that prior to his initial meeting with Fielder, he had given little thought to such matters.

Henderson said that he next encountered Fielder when he was a student at Berkeley, which was home to countless progressive social movements, including the Free Speech Movement, the Anti-War Movement, the Civil Rights Movement, the Black Power Movement, the Feminist Movement, and the Environmental Movement. The City of Berkeley had elected three city council members who were referred to as the radical three: Ilona Hancock, Ira Simmons, and D'Army Bailey. Henderson was an intern with Bailey's office. When all three faced a recall election, Fielder spoke out publicly against the recall efforts and later condemned the successful recall of D'Army Bailey. Henderson remembered being impressed with the position Fielder took in the recall election. He said, "Black folks of her generation were rather suspicious of these radicals, who they thought were too far to the left, but not Marie Fielder." Fielder also supported Ron Dellums, a Berkeley City Council member and member of the Black Panther Party, who later served as a US congressman and mayor of Oakland.

When Henderson joined the faculty of the University of San Francisco, he was also appointed to the board of the Westside Mental Health Center. He recalled a day when Marie Fielder came to the center and gave several members of the board "absolute hell." She said, "I see you fellows have started a new organization, the National Association of Black Psychologists. Wonderful, but you've got to interact with mainstream psychologists at some point. If your plan doesn't include for some interaction or confrontation with them, then your mission is in vain." The group Fielder chastised included prominent African American psychologists, including William Grier and Price Cobbs (1968), who authored the influential book *Black Rage*. One of the psychologists said, "Dr. Fielder, I have a doctorate too. You must have a problem." Fielder retorted, "I think your doctorate is your problem. You need to think about what a doctorate really equips you to do and whether you are moving in the right direction." Henderson said he remembers that exchange as though it happened yesterday, just as he remembers encountering Fielder again when he joined the faculty of Fielding Graduate University in 1991. When Fielder saw him at Fielding, she approached him with a big smile on her face, and exclaimed, "you again!"

Lenneal Henderson also shared his knowledge of the community meetings Fielder had in the aftermath of the Birmingham Church Bombing in 1963 and Dr. King's assassination in 1968. During those meetings, Fielder used her formidable intergroup dialogue skills to soothe racial tensions. Some in the African American community condemned her for her efforts, claiming that people were entitled to their anger and needed to express it in any way they saw fit. Fielder responded, "We have to maintain a moral high ground here, so that we will have a reserve of credibility when we get back on the streets to protest for our rights again." In some ways, Fielder's remarks on the response of the African American community to violence perpetrated by White supremacists foreshadowed Michelle Obama's famous refrain, "When they go low, we go high."

Marie Fielder in the early 1960's (*Courtesy, Nicola Smith*).

## CHAPTER 2

## INTERGROUP DIALOGUE AND DESEGREGATION IN CALIFORNIA PUBLIC SCHOOLS

Marie Fielder was completing her doctoral work at the University of Chicago when the U.S. Supreme Court issued its landmark decision in *Brown v Board of Education* in 1954. The *Brown* decision struck at the heart of institutionalized racism in the American South by declaring racially segregated schools unconstitutional. The decision sent shockwaves across the South, spurring a new wave of White Southern backlash against all attempts to achieve racial equality (Dittmer, 1995). Efforts to integrate Southern schools met with widespread resistance. In 1957, Arkansas Governor Orval Faubus deployed the National Guard to prevent nine African American students from entering Central High School in Little Rock (Anderson, 2004). Two years later, in Prince Edward County, Virginia, public officials elected to close all public schools rather than comply with a federal court order to integrate them (Green, 2015).

Public schools outside of the South, where school segregation was not mandated but resulted from widespread residential segregation, also struggled with White resistance to integration in varying degrees. In May 1964, the Board of Education in Berkeley, California, approved a plan to desegregate all junior high schools. Shortly thereafter, members of the Board of Education faced a recall election, which failed when 62 percent of voters opposed the recall measure. In 1968, the Berkeley Unified School District (BUSD) gained the distinction of becoming the first city outside of the South to willingly desegregate its schools. In contrast, Boston erupted with violent demonstrations in response to the school board's plan to integrate schools, a plan which involved the implementation of a busing program that would transport students outside of their racially segregated neighborhoods (Reed, 1982).

Successful school integration was more than a matter of reordering student populations so that the racial composition of each school generally mirrored that of the school district. Rather, truly integrated schools also required a racially diverse staff, faculty, and administration, as well as a redesigned curriculum that did not focus solely on the experience of White people. Although her significant contributions to school desegregation are undocumented, Marie Fielder proved instrumental in the desegregation of the BUSD and integration of schools throughout California. The history of school desegregation continues to be relevant, not only because schools in the United States never achieved the level of racial integration promised by *Brown* (Noguera, 1994), but also because the method of intergroup dialogue employed by Fielder throughout her career has the potential to address the racial tensions that continue to plague the country.

**The Desegregation of the Berkeley Unified School District**
The successful desegregation of the Berkeley Unified School

District in 1968 resulted from nearly a decade of study, workshops, and planning. [4] In January 1958, the local chapter of the National Association for the Advancement of Colored People (NAACP) gave a presentation to the Berkeley Board of Education regarding racial inequality in the BUSD. The board subsequently passed a motion to appoint a Citizens' Committee to study the issue, and the Committee reported their findings to the board in 1959. The Citizens' Committee concluded that the board had an obligation to address racial inequity within in the BUSD and recommended reforms pertaining to student discipline, career counseling, racial composition of staff, parental involvement, and the grievance process. The committee also recommended that the board provide intergroup education for school staff, faculty, and administration. It further recommended the creation of a standing citizens' advisory committee to advise the board on interracial relations (Favors, 1969).

Following the Citizens' Committee's recommendation, in early 1961, the superintendent of the BUSD invited Marie Fielder to serve as an intergroup education consultant to the district. Fielder's initial step in assisting the BUSD with understanding and addressing racial inequity involved inviting members of a junior high school to participate in an intergroup education study. The junior high school she approached drew students from elementary schools in two distinct areas of Berkeley; one area was predominantly White, and the other was predominantly African American. Because the racial composition of the elementary schools was still determined by de facto segregation in 1961, the students had no opportunity for interracial interaction prior to beginning junior high. Fielder invited the 10 staff members who decided to participate in the study to use a tape recorder to record their concerns regarding the academic achievement of the students who previously attended the predominantly African American elementary school. Staff members voiced concerns regarding students' feelings about their education, their grades, and their teachers. The staff members who participated in the study shared their findings with teachers from the elementary school. The study participants and teachers worked collaboratively to develop a survey which they administered to the junior high school students and used the survey results to assess and make relevant changes to the school curriculum. Under Fielder's direction, a group of elementary school teachers followed a similar protocol to investigate the attitudes of the parents whose children attended their school (Favors, 1969).

Later that year, Fielder organized a voluntary seminar in intergroup education for BUSD staff. A group of 15 people, including teachers, administrators, and guidance counselors, met over the course of a school year. The group initially met in school classrooms but later met in members' homes.[5] An example of the group's process is illustrative of Fielder's methods (Favors, 1969). She provided each member of the group with a copy of *Knock on Any Door*, a novel by Willard Motley (1989). Originally published in 1947, Motley's novel follows the story of Nick Romano, a teenage immigrant whose father loses their family business. As a result of his father's financial difficulties, Nick struggles to find a path toward the American Dream promised to immigrants. He commits several petty crimes and is sent to a reform school. As an adult, he stands trial for the murder of a police officer. The novel is a study in the influence of economic inequality on the trajectory of an individual's life. and Fielder used *Knock on*

*Any Door* as the lynchpin of a technique that she described as "the novel as teacher." After group members read the novel, Fielder distributed a series of educational books that related to the central struggles that Nick experiences and asked group members to identify interventions that could have been used to alter Nick's fate (Favors, 1969).

By June 1962, 120 staff members had registered for the upcoming intergroup education seminar. Fielder decided that without funding for paid group leaders, members of the 1961 Intergroup Education Project would be divided into triads to serve as group leaders. Fielder assigned each member of a triad a specific role. The triad leader would serve as a group antagonist who challenged group assumptions. The group interpreter would help them clarify their ideas, and another member would serve to soothe tensions within the group as they arose. Fielder provided several trainings for the triads; they would subsequently lead nine small groups throughout 1962. The 1961 Intergroup Education Project cohort also developed a broad proposal designed to create opportunities for interaction among students from across the BUSD. Their proposal included a recommendation for an all-city orchestra, an all-city newspaper, an all-city choral group, and interschool clubs. Fielder continued to serve as a consultant to the BUSD through 1969. Each year, paid staff was allocated to assist her in developing what eventually became the Berkeley Unified School District Office of Human Relations. During the 1968-1969 school year, seven paid staff members worked under her direction (Favors, 1969).

Harriet Jenkins, a BUSD administer who helped achieve desegregation within the district and later served as the assistant administrator for the equal opportunity office of

NASA, summarized the pivotal role that Fielder played in the desegregation of the district, recalling that,

> "the preparation and the care that went into [desegregation] was absolutely unbelievable. I give credit to Dr. Marie Fielder. She worked with our board, our community, adults, parents, teachers, administrators, and students to help us prepare for the K-6 desegregation move. The sum total of all that effort was to say, "Hey, this is what we want to do, and these are the reasons we want to do it. We need your best minds and concerns to be brought to the forefront. You can disagree with us, just bring us your concerns"." (National Aeronautics and Space Administration, 2011)

As Jenkins' recollection suggests, part of Fielder's ability to build connection among racially diverse groups lay in her willingness to invite dissension as an initial step toward unity.

BUSD has been able to ensure continued racial and socioeconomic diversity in its schools despite challenges. In 1996, California voters passed Proposition 209, which prohibited considerations of race, sex, or ethnicity within government organizations, including public schools. Some White residents of Berkeley used Proposition 209 to challenge BUSD's school zoning plan. They argued that the district could not consider students' race or ethnic background when assigning them to a school. The California Appellate Court ruled that because the BUSD zoning plan combines elements of school choice with geographically based zoning that considers the overall demographic characteristics of a neighborhood as opposed to an individual student's race or ethnicity, the plan does not violate Proposition 209 (Chavez & Frankenberg, 2009).

**Desegregation of Richmond Unified School District**

Marie Fielder once said, "If I always had three jobs, it was only because I couldn't get five" (N. Smith, personal communication, June 12, 2021). The truth of her statement is borne out by her desegregation work in the Richmond Unified School District (RUSD), which she undertook while simultaneously serving as a consultant to BUSD. Fielder's work with Richmond was established upon the intergroup education model that she had developed within BUSD. She continued to focus on helping students, faculty, and community members in cultivating interpersonal relationships needed to support desegregation efforts. She also began introducing school communities to literature that addressed "grouping practices, intelligence, testing, discipline, teaching the disadvantaged, desegregation, integration, race and race relations" (Fielder & Dyckman, 1967, p. 155). As she had done in Berkeley, Fielder taught members of RUSD that a truly integrated school included a curriculum, staff, teachers, and administrators that reflected the diversity in the racial backgrounds of a desegregated student body. Fielder based her framework for work with RUSD on the district's development history. Likewise, this history is relevant and provided in the following paragraphs.

Richmond sits on the eastern shore of the San Francisco Bay area in Contra Costa County. Prior to World War II, the small city had a population of approximately 20,000 people, most of whom worked in local industries, which included manufacturing and oil refineries. World War II brought a significant expansion of nearby shipyards, and the influx of workers needed to fill newly created jobs, which resulted in the quadrupling of the population in ten years (Kirp et al., 1979). The racial demographics of Richmond also shifted dramatically during the 1940s. Between 1940 and 1947, the African American population increased from one percent of the total population to 14 percent (Wilson, 1967).

Since the city's founding, the African American community has been segregated from the White community, and the increase in the African American population during World War II was not welcomed by the White community. Signs reading, "Negro patrons not wanted" became commonplace in White-owned businesses (Wilson, 1967, p. 304). In the early 1950s, Whites began leaving Richmond and relocating to nearby communities. Their destinations depended largely on their socioeconomic status. More financially well-off Whites moved to the foothill communities of El Cerrito and Kensington, while working class Whites moved to the new communities of Pinole and El Sobrante. The subsequent change in the racial demographics of Richmond meant that the city was 41 percent African American by 1975 (Kirp et al., 1979).

The shifting racial demographics of Richmond and the surrounding communities led to de facto segregation within Contra Costra County. Consequently, because only a few Whites were bothered by this fact, all five communities were joined in a single school district in 1964. In 1965, the local chapter of the Congress of Racial Equality (CORE) gave a presentation to the school board outlining the extent of de facto racial segregation in RUSD elementary schools and demanded that the board take immediate steps to integrate all public schools. In response to CORE's demands, on September 1, 1965, the school board passed a resolution acknowledging de facto segregation in RUSD. The resolution noted that such segregation was one of the central problems facing urban school districts, and the board committed to taking steps to achieve racial parity in all RUSD schools (Fielder & Dyckman, 1967). The school board subsequently appointed a citizens' advisory committee to study the issue of racial inequality in RUSD and to make recommendations regarding desegregation (Kirp et al., 1979). As the Berkeley Board of Education had established previously, the Richmond school board also funded an intergroup education program and appointed Marie Fielder as director.

Fielder's work with RUSD involved the development and implementation of two intergroup dialogue programs. [5] The programs were supported by funding from the Elementary and Secondary Education Act of 1965. Fielder referred to each program as a "Leadership Training Institute in the Problems of School Desegregation." Fielder's first Institute in RUSD was held in 1966. One of the primary accomplishments of the 1966 Institute was the creation of the Intergroup In-Service Education Center, which received $35,000 in funding for the RUSD. The center's primary mission was to provide additional education for school staff regarding intergroup concerns and to serve as a model for the translation of civil rights law into action. Following the conclusion of the formal program of the 1966 Institute, participants continued to attend follow-up meetings throughout the 1966-1967 academic year.

Planning for the 1967 Institute coincided with the final meeting of the 1966 cohort. Gertrude Noar, a nationally recognized consultant on school desegregation and staff member of both the 1966 and 1967 Institutes, was a featured speaker at that meeting. Noar emphasized the need for the 1967 Institute to continue the work begun during the 1966 Institute so that RUSD could avoid sporadic, disjointed efforts as it moved toward desegregation, and she encouraged participants of the 1966 institute to become involved in the recruitment and orientation of 1967 Institute participants.

In April 1967, Institute staff held a two-day workshop to discuss the format of the upcoming Institute, and they invited potential Institute applicants to attend and learn more about the goals of the program. Clyde DeBerry, a noted authority on racial issues in education, provided a keynote address focusing on the report issued by the Citizens' Advisory Committee on de facto segregation. The April meetings were the first opportunity to for interested alumni of the 1966 Institute to assume a leadership role in planning for the 1967 Institute, and they served as chairs for small group discussions involving potential 1967 Institute participants.

Marie Fielder held the first formal meetings for the 1967 Institute in May. Institute participants included teachers, counselors, administrators, school board members, and community members. RUSD students were also invited to participate. Prior to the May meetings, RUSD Superintendent Denzil Widel held a conference for leaders within the school system to address the question, "What Do <u>We</u> Do About the Defacto Segregation Report" (Fielder & Dyckman, 1967, p. 42). Over 100 RUSD staff members attended the conference. White community members, upset about the school district resources spent on the conference, called a meeting to discuss their concerns, and the scheduled meeting coincided with the Institute's orientation meeting. Institute staff amended the agenda for the orientation to include a field trip to the community meeting where Institute participants could "observe the forces of segregation and disintegration at work" (p. 42). Participants had the opportunity to discuss their observations during the June 1967 meetings, which were facilitated by Elias Blake, who served as an evaluator of civil rights programs throughout the United States.

Student participants were offered an additional orientation, which also occurred in June. Students had participated in the 1966 Institute but had served an ancillary role. In contrast, the 1967 Institute considered students full participants and paid them the same $15 per day stipend other Institute participants received. It quickly became evident that students had little opportunity for interracial interaction prior to the orientation sessions. White students initially reported that they harbored no racial prejudice toward African American students, but their attitudes began to shift after the African American students began to meet separately with the approval of the group leader. At this point in the Institute, one White student said he "could accept Black Power and Black Identity intellectually, but it was still difficult to understand and accept it emotionally" (Berry, 1967, p. 251). In response to the anger African American students expressed as the discrimination they routinely encountered, several White students said that they had not expected the orientation to be so traumatic.

The Institute itself consisted of two 10-day programs. The first began on Friday, June 23, 1967, at Helms Junior High in Richmond. Superintendent Widel opened the session with a speech positioning the Institute as a joint venture of local, state, and national governments, and several days of the Institute were devoted to addresses by various government officials on the importance of school integration. On Sunday, the participants were given the day off, and Marie Fielder invited members of the RUSD Board of Education and influential community members to meet Institute staff.

The following Saturday, students were excused while adult participants attended a sensitivity training. Over the course of the previous week, the students had voiced their concerns over the quality of the education they were receiving and teachers who did not seem to care about them. It became evident to the teachers present, who heard intelligent students use limited vocabularies and poor grammar to articulate their ideas, that the students had received a substandard education. Still, the teachers struggled to engage directly with the students. In their description of the Institute proceedings, Fielder and Dyckman (1967) noted that "Teachers came prepared to talk about students, but not the students." Similarly, most of the adult participants, "were prepared to discuss desegregation but found it difficult and a learning task to be segregated along lines of generation, color, social class, and social assignment" (p. 48). Nevertheless, Fielder maintained that school staff and community members could not expect to integrate schools successfully if they remained unwilling to listen to students' concerns.

Following the 10-day workshop at Helms Junior High, the Institute hosted a 10-day residential program at Notre Dame School, an all-girls, Catholic, college prep school. According to a report summarizing the work of the Institute, the residential program was an important part of the Institute's design. The shared meals and living spaces afforded participants many opportunities for informal conversations, supporting the Institute's overarching goal of replicating the daily, commonplace interactions among interracial groups of students and faculty so that participants would have experience navigating interracial relationships before school desegregation was formally implemented. The Institute focused on intergroup dialogue, but it also included discussions of an integrated curriculum that recognized the contributions of people of color as well the formation of student groups that would support specific races and ethnicities such as a Black Student Association.

During the residential program, Institute staff member, Dr. Clyde DeBerry, a professor at the University of Oregon and CORE leader, gave an address arguing in favor of Black separatism. Calling for the renaming of predominately African American schools in honor of Black leaders and encouraging the creation of school holidays to commemorate significant moments in Black history, DeBerry said schools must be taken away from "whitey." He added "Unless changes are made in the decision-making process, there will be trouble. Black people are tired of being kicked in the butt. Black schools are for Black people and therefore must be controlled by Black people" (Fielder & Dyckman, 1967, p. 53).

Fielder recalled that the cross racial confrontation that followed Dr. DeBerry's speech created some anxiety for her and challenged Institute staff and participants to explore the extent to which their support for school desegregation went beyond mere words. African American participants met separately to discuss their reactions to the ideas advanced by Dr. DeBerry, forcing the remaining participants to reflect on their commitment to racial equality. Fielder responded to the interracial tension by facilitating a large group discussion to address it directly. Although she worried about the possibility of continued conflict, she found that participants were honest and insightful in their reflections. She noted, "In the days following the emotional catharsis of the heated exchange, interpersonal friendships and interracial understanding continued to grow, but this time, on a more sound, and open basis" (p. 55).

Additional interracial conflict emerged regarding the Institute's treatment of Latinx communities. On the opening day of the Institute, Lawrence Gonzales of the United Council of Spanish Speaking Organizations accused the Institute of discriminating against "Spanish speaking persons" noting that only two community representatives and two students with "Spanish surnames" were participating in the Institute (Fielder & Dyckman, 1967, p. 259). Fielder forwarded Gonzales' formal letter of complaint to the U.S. Department of Education and the San Francisco Office of Equal Employment Opportunities, and representatives of both organizations contacted her. In response, Fielder provided documentation of the efforts the Institute had made to recruit members of the Spanish speaking community. She argued that the Institute's involvement with the Spanish speaking community was "more extensive than it may appear to be when viewed solely in terms of participant numbers," and she highlighted Spanish speaking representation among Institute staff and invited guest speakers to support her claim (Fielder & Dyckman, 1967, p. 260).

While Fielder defended the Institute against claims of discrimination, she also appeared to use the accusation as an opportunity to reflect on the Institute's practices. In responding to Gonzales' claim, she wrote,

"It is always advisable and democratic for each public undertaking or enterprise to check itself on the in-process treatment of minorities. It is much too easy to make statements or to write proposals articulating democratic intentions. Mr. Gonzales' charge has given us opportunity to evaluate our day-to-day behavior and our entire operations.

We are not reprimanded by what we review. Neither are we finished or satisfied; we intend to be even more aggressive in recruitment of Spanish-speaking participants and give more depth to our inclusion of the concerns of Spanish speaking citizens" (Fielder & Dyckman, 1967, pp. 264-265).

There are some aspects of Fielder's statement that are problematic when viewed through the lens of a 21st century analysis of race. Her use of the term "Spanish speaking" to refer to a group of people we might currently refer to as Latinx is somewhat unsettling, although it appears to have been the preferred term at the time, because it glosses over the diversity of the Latinx community. Nevertheless, there may be a dimension of the conflict between the Latinx community and the Institute that is illustrative of race relations during the late 1960s. As Behnken (2004) notes, "black-brown relations in the U.S., especially during the civil rights era, could be both conflicted and cooperative, contentious and collaborative" (p. 4). As cross racial alliances have expanded, the narrative of race relations in the United States, which has historically been framed as an issue of Black and White, has been challenged. One of the enduring contributions of Fielder's work is the commitment she demonstrated to on-going dialogue across difference, and her career was marked by willingness to engage in difficult conversations. If you had a genuine concern, Marie Fielder wanted to talk with you about it.

Two thirds of the way through the residential program, the Institute hosted a Visitation Day, during which it opened its door to the families of participants as well as business, social, and educational leaders. Visitors were invited to join the smaller working groups within the Institute, and they learned the specifics of and rational for the various proposals developed by the Institute. Visitation day not only built support for the Institute's work within the larger community, it also helped to dispel rumors that the Institute operated in secrecy in order to protect its plans to advance proposal tailored to meet the needs of a select few.

During the residential program, Institute staff also worked with participants to produce a daily newsletter, *The Belmont Barb*. Participants used the newsletter to publish their reactions to invited speakers and reflections on the progress of the Institute. On July 7th, several African American students proposed a three-part plan to promote cross-racial dialogue among students. The plan suggested the creation of an "Afro-American Student Association" which would strategically partner with White students to promote the interests of both groups. White students would also work separately in White communities. The final part of the proposal would involve the creation of an interracial council at every high school.

Throughout the Institute, participants met in subgroups to discuss issues related to their specific roles and interests. By the end of the Institute, each subgroup had prepared a report outlining specific proposals and the rationale for them. Fielder included these reports in the document she prepared for the

Department of Education. As the Institute drew to close, participants reflected on their experiences. One participant spoke positively of his time at the Institute, writing, "I enjoyed working with you and the wonderful people in Richmond. It was an experience I will treasure. I believe that there are people in the Richmond Schools willing to deal effectively with school desegregation" (Fielder & Dyckman, 1967, p. 188). Another participant was less flattering of the Institute's work and less optimistic about its long term impact: "As for the institute being used as a de facto segregation change agent, realistically may be difficult to predict, given the type of leadership program and the selection of participants" (p. 191).

The available archival sources indicate that Fielder's work with RUSD concluded before the school board addressed desegregation in a comprehensive manner. In 1969, the school board of RUSD voted, three to two, to implement a desegregation plan over the objections of many White parents. The liberal-leaning board recognized the likely political consequences of their decision, and they worked with local attorneys to obtain a court decree, which they hoped would prevent their decision from being overturned. Three weeks later, the school board members who had voted in support of the desegregation plan were recalled and replaced with a conservative majority. The court order they hoped would ensure the long-term viability of the desegregation was deemed unenforceable, and the new board members quickly voted to overturn the previous board's desegregation plan. Despite this significant setback, the new, conservative board quickly adopted a Richmond Integration Plan, which permitted students to transfer to another school within the district. Students opting to participate in this plan were provided with school-funded busing. Although the Richmond Integration Plan reduced de facto segregation within the RUSD to a degree, students attending predominately African American schools continued to receive a lower-quality education (Kirp et al., 1979).

Marie Fielder likely felt some disappointment that RUSD did not ultimately opt for district wide desegregation, but I would suggest that the foundations of interracial dialogue she laid during the 1966 and 1967 Institutes helped persuade conservative board members that some action should be taken to address the educational disparities among schools experiencing de facto desegregation. The Richmond Integration Plan was a step toward integration, albeit a very small one. As her friend and colleague Anna DiStefano recalled, "Marie saw the struggle for racial equality as the work of several lifetimes," and Fielder's work in BUSD and RUSD had moved the long arc of racial justice forward.

Marie Fielder's work to desegregate California school continued well into the 1970s. In 1968, she served on a committee convened by the California State Department of Education, Office of Compensatory Education, Bureau of Intergroup Relations and helped to develop *A Manual for the Evaluation of Desegregation in California Public Schools*. In addition to outlining a 12-stage model for school desegregation, the manual describes the way in which the desegregation model was implemented in Riverside, California (Mercer, 1968). Throughout her career, Fielder's used the intergroup education model she had developed during her desegregation work as a template for the consulting services she provided to school districts, municipalities, and corporations across the United States.

Marie Fielder in the late 1960's (*Courtesy, Nicola Smith*).

# Chapter 3

# Increasing Equity in Schools, Municipalities, and Corporate America

Marie Fielder's daughter, Nicola Smith, recalled that her mother's first scholarly love was school climate and school culture. As Fielder's career progressed, her professional work began to overlap with the work of the Civil Rights Movement. The intersection of Fielder's work on school culture with the Civil Rights Movement is evident in her efforts to support school integration through the use of intergroup dialogue. Fielder's reputation as a skilled trainer on interracial relations began to grow, and from the early 1960s on, her consulting services focused almost exclusively on what would now be termed equity, diversity, and inclusion, but was then called human relations training. She continued to work with schools, and her consulting work expanded to include corporations, law enforcement, non-profits, and municipalities.

Fielder was a consummate networker and a very successful consultant. Early in her career, she joined several professional organizations, including the Association of Supervision and Curriculum Development (ASCD), the American Educational Research Association (AERA), and several others. Smith recalled that in 1960, when the average annual household income was $15,000, Marie Fielder was earning $60,000 a year, which would equate to approximately $600,000 in 2022. Fielder once had difficulty paying taxes on her income because the tax preparer refused to believe that an African American woman could have such a lucrative career.

The true scope of Fielder's consulting work would be impossible to capture within the confines of this monograph. However, to illustrate her consulting work, I focus on three vignettes. The first is taken from an interview of Nicola Smith with one of her mother's mentees, John Stromberg, who recalls the way in which his work with Fielder influenced his work. Two additional vignettes focus on consulting Fielder's work with the Elk Grove Unified School District and the Travis Unified School District to understand and improve the culture of the schools within those districts.

## My Mentees are My Manuscripts

Chapter 1 reveals that Marie Fielder published very little during her career. She once explained this fact to her daughter, stating, "My mentees are my manuscripts." One notable mentee was John Stromberg, a corporate consultant who later served as the mayor of the City of Ashland in southern Oregon. Stromberg met Fielder in the late 1970s, when they were both invited to participate in a discussion group operated by the Center for Designed Change in Mill Valley, California. Stromberg recalled that meeting Marie Fielder was akin to meeting a celebrity. Shortly before their first meeting, Fielder had been invited to become a candidate for superintendent of public instruction for the state of California, an opportunity that she declined. Stromberg said, "Meeting Marie represented the big leagues for me."

## Chapter 3: Increasing Equity in Schools, Municipalities and Corporate America

In describing his work with Fielder at the Center for Designed Change, Stromberg remembered:

> "Marie really didn't get interested until there was movement going on in the dynamic. I sometimes thought Marie was bored until the shit hit the fan. Then she would move into action with gusto and enthusiasm. Her presence, her intelligence, and her insight were never intrusive, and it was never something objectionable. She just took over."

Stromberg learned a tremendous amount from Fielder's method of group intervention. He then applied it to his own work. He recalled a specific incident in which Fielder's influence proved pivotal.

The incident involved a training that Stromberg designed while he was working as an internal organizational development consultant for a telephone company in California. The company decided to cross-train customer service representatives in an effort to increase productivity, and they needed to develop a program for training each representative to help customers establish new service, address billing problems, and reconnect their phone service. The company's strategy involved having representatives train each other. Representatives whose primary task was taking new customer orders trained those who resolved billing problems and vice versa. At the time, having representatives train their peers, rather than relying on a professional trainer or supervisor to conduct the training, was controversial. Yet, Stromberg's training pushed the boundaries even further, when he decided to allow mid-range and poor performing employees to train their peers, rather than having the top performing employees lead the training. Stromberg recalled, "It was wild and crazy. It was an experiment, but I couldn't resist it."

The pilot version of the training program worked well but was limited to a very small group of people. As the program expanded, it began to encounter difficulties because the top performing representatives responsible for taking new orders was having to learn from the poorest-performing billing representative. Stromberg noted, "This is where I turned to the skills that Marie Fielder had taught me. I did something that I would only have done because I'd seen Marie do it."

Stromberg talked with each of the representatives separately and then scheduled a meeting. Almost all the service representatives were women in those days. About 50 percent of the representatives were African American and the other 50 percent belonged to various other racial and ethnic groups. The woman who had first complained to Stromberg about the training program was Puerto Rican. She was a high-performing employee, and she was having trouble with a shy, African American woman, named Gina, who lacked confidence in her ability to perform her job. Stromberg started off the group not knowing what to say and realized his situation was similar to those in which he had seen Marie Fielder thrive. He grounded himself in the reality of the situation and was able to draw on his professional experience as he thought about what to say. The words eventually came to him. Stromberg said that as he navigated that situation, he thought of Fielder, "She would have had the nerve to do it. She would have done it beautifully. It was almost as though she couldn't work unless there was a high conflict situation. That's where she did her best work."

Stromberg said that he told the gathered employees that

## Chapter 3: Increasing Equity in Schools, Municipalities and Corporate America

there is one person in every group who is very much in touch with their feelings, more so than anybody else in the group. That person sometimes takes on and carries the emotional burden for the entire group. It becomes the group's responsibility to support that person because they are taking responsibility for the emotions of the entire group. Stromberg didn't mention the person he was referencing by name, but everyone knew he was talking about Gina. He was legitimizing Gina and who she was, and the group bought into to what he was saying. Stromberg added, "It was a very Marie thing to do."

Stromberg recalled that Gina brightened up considerably after that meeting. One day, he got a call from her direct supervisor. She told him that Gina's performance had improved dramatically, but the supervisor had a problem. She had to give Gina a performance review that covered the previous six months. Prior to Stromberg's intervention, Gina's performance had been awful. Her supervisor said, "Gina was incompetent, unwilling, disrespectful, and just terrible. Now she's really trying. She's a different person. She's doing so well." The supervisor knew she had to give Gina an honest review, but she knew Gina was very sensitive. The supervisor was concerned that a negative performance review could destroy Gina's self-confidence at a time when she was making a wonderful change.

Stromberg said he did not offer the supervisor a specific solution to her problem because he had learned from Fielder that sometimes the best way to help someone was to allow them to talk through the problem. By the end of the conversation, the supervisor said she had figured how to approach the evaluation.

The supervisor contacted Stromberg a few weeks later.

She told him that she could not believe what happened. Gina came in for her review, but before the supervisor could say anything, Gina said, "I know my performance was really awful for most of the review period." She described all the awful things she had done. Gina added, "I feel terrible about that performance, but I have a new approach to what I'm doing. I love my work. Everything is working well for me." Gina said she would not object in any way if her supervisor included her poor performance in the evaluation. The customer service representatives were unionized, and they had the right to file a grievance if they received a negative review. Gina had voluntarily given herself a negative review, and her supervisor reveled at Gina's willingness to honestly review her work.

John recalled that Gina had been assigned to a specific training group because her performance was so poor. Everybody thought she was dumb, but she wasn't dumb. She was actually a person of special character that the group managed to awaken. Everyone supported her, and she changed because of the group's involvement.

### Elk Grove School District

Elk Grove, California, which is located to the south of Sacramento, was undergoing a dramatic shift in racial demographics in the late 1970s. Prior to this demographic shift, Elk Grove Unified School District (EGUSD), which serves Elk Grove and parts of Rancho Cordova, Sacramento, and unincorporated Sacramento County, was historically a predominantly White district. During the late 1970s, the district experienced a significant increase in the enrollment of students of color and began having problems with race relations. To address the increase in racial tension, Dr. Glenn

Hood, the superintendent of EGUSD, hired Marie Field to serve as a consultant to the district on human relations.

Beverly Palley was one of the few female African American teachers in EGUSD in 1979. She taught math at the newly constructed Valley High School and had two young children who attended elementary school in the district. A recent transplant from the Bay Area, Palley was comfortable with living and working in a racially diverse community, and she had taken several Black studies courses while pursuing her undergraduate degree at California State University Hayward (now California State University, East Bay). Palley was initially puzzled by the racial tension in EGUSD and noted that many in the school district were upset by the changes in racial demographics among the student population. White teachers experienced the most difficulty because they had never worked with students of color. The White teachers were not open to change, but Palley saw it as her duty as a teacher to be open to racial diversity. Palley recalled, "My teaching credential was in mathematics. It didn't say anything about whether I was supposed to teach black, red, green, or white students. It said teach mathematics to students. I wanted other teachers to feel the same way."

Palley recalled the first time she met Marie Fielder, who arrived at the EGUSD Administrative Office driving the family station wagon with her mother, Ellee, in the backseat. Fielder brought her mother to Elk Grove each time she visited, and Palley noted that Fielder often concluded a day's session with the observation, "Mother is at the hotel. I've got to get back to her." Palley never met Ellee, but she imagined that some of tremendous wisdom and compassion Marie Fielder exuded came from her mother.

Palley summarized her first impression of Fielder in a single word, "Wow!" She added that she had never encountered a professional of her caliber or an African American woman who rivaled Fielder. "She was smart. She was down to earth. She was open. She would say what was on her mind. She was an inspirational person." Palley said she modeled the example set by Fielder, who taught her to be the person she is today.

Palley's commitment to racial equality, combined with her admiration for Marie Fielder, inspired her to pursue a leadership role in the human relations program that Fielder had developed, and she volunteered to serve as one of 20 lead learners, who would guide the district in the months between Fielder's visits. EGUSD offered Fielder a three-year contract and paid her $15,000 per year for her services. Initially, many people in EGUSD resisted Fielder's involvement in their district. Palley recalled that other teachers became upset when they discovered Fielder's salary, and they wondered why she was so highly paid. In Palley's view, Fielder's identity as an African American woman played a central role in the outrage that the teachers expressed. Palley responded to the teachers' complaints by saying that Fielder was needed to bring humanity to the entire district, and her services were needed to unite students, parents, teachers, staff, and administrators. Resistance to Fielder's work dissipated as members of the district got to know her and experience her capacity to empathize with them across their differences.

During her tenure as an educational consultant to EGUSD, Fielder visited the district three to four times per year. Each of her visits lasted three days. During her visits, Fielder presented on issues relevant to improving human relations within the district and met with the lead learners. The lead learners would report on the activity and progress of the smaller groups under their supervision, and Fielder would introduce new methods and exercises that they could use with their groups over a three-month period. Palley recalled that Fielder was very kind to the lead learners even as she was encouraging them to think deeply about complex issues and methods. These same issues and methods would be used by lead learners as they engaged the members of their small groups.

Fielder would meet with students during the day, and she would work with teachers and staff in the evening. Palley recalled that the focus of those meetings was learning to work with parents. Fielder facilitated discussions on racial disparities within the district, asking why African American students were suspended more frequently than White students. Fielder also met with a group of concerned African American parents, and Beverly Palley appreciated the opportunity to engage with Fielder as both a high school teacher and a parent of children attending elementary schools in the district. She recalled several conversations between the two of them that began with Marie Fielder saying, "Beverly, this is what we need to do to get the school district going."

Beverly Palley did not learn of Fielder's connection to Fielding Graduate University until she enrolled in the Educational Leadership for Change doctoral program in 1998 and became reacquainted with her. Fielder remembered Palley and the work they had done together in Elk Grove. Palley said that when she met Fielder again in 1998, "She was still the same person I had met in 1979. She was still eager, still supportive." Palley recalled that Fielder and the curriculum she helped develop at Fielding focused on structural inequalities and methods for bringing about systemic changes. While completing her doctoral studies, Palley worked part-time for the Oakland Unified School District and part-time for Project Pipeline, an alternative teacher certification program. After graduation, she became a professor of education at Alliant International University. Palley provided an example of how she applied what Fielder had taught her to work with students at Alliant, where she was employed, in the integration of interpersonal relationships and structural inequality to effect racial equality in an educational setting.

At Alliant, Palley was tasked with supervising teachers, many of whom were White and had graduated recently from Ivy League schools. She worked to prepare the teachers for employment in the Oakland Unified School District. She recalled working with a student she referred to as Jane, who was a high school science teacher. As part of her supervisory responsibilities, Palley would observe Jane teaching, but during one observation session, Jane was not really teaching. Jane had a PowerPoint presentation, and her teaching method consisted of little more than reading what she had written on each slide before clicking to the next one.

After the observation session, Palley said, "Okay Jane, we need to talk about what I observed. I really didn't observe you doing anything except reading from your slides." Palley went on to point out that one student was sleeping while another was combing her hair. She asked Jane how she could engage her students in the actual learning process, and she told her it was her responsibility to circulate around the classroom — to talk to her students, to ask questions. Jane had done none of that. She just relied on her PowerPoint slides, while her students were doing whatever they pleased. Palley told Jane, "It was very frustrating for me as your professor to come and watch you do this."

Palley said that she did not want to interrupt Jane's class to critique her teaching method because she did not want to embarrass her, and she had not previously discussed with her the possibility of interrupting class before the observation session began. Instead, Palley said that she relied on what Marie Fielder had taught her regarding structural inequality, and she would often supervise her students by going into their classrooms to work as a demonstrating teacher. Palley said that her students frequently complained that she was a more effective teacher because both she and they were African American. However, Palley said, it was not helpful to view the situation through that lens. Rather, Jane's students were the instructors for their teachers, and it was their obligation to find a way to engage the students' interest. In other words, the students were the instructors, and the instructors were the students. Palley said she would review the six domains that formed the standards for teachers in California with her students, and ask, how do you engage? How do you deliver the lesson? How do you make the students self-directed learners?

For Palley, the example she relayed was fundamentally about structural inequality because the White teachers expected their students to understand the material through the eyes of the teacher, when the teachers should be trying to view the material from the perspective of their students, finding ways to make the lessons relevant to their students' lives. Palley said that she sometimes got into trouble with her students, who would write on their course evaluations, "Dr. Palley always talks about race." Palley said she did emphasize race because the teachers she trained were "working with my little brothers and sisters" who were not paying attention.

She told them that talking about race in the classroom was something she felt she had to do.

Palley said that while she was teaching at Alliant, she created a course in urban education. Her course was a master's level course, but she always believed it should be a course that was required of students before they obtained their teaching credentials. Palley believed that developing a proficiency in working with diverse learners was an essential part of becoming an effective teacher. Additionally, she maintained that her work with Marie Fielder had played a pivotal role in her decision to develop that course, adding, "I still carry Marie with me in my heart."

### Travis Unified School District

Throughout her long career, Marie Fielder remained consistent in her desire to facilitate change in school culture to promote racial equality. In 1994, at the age of 77, she accepted a two-year contract with the Travis Unified School District (TUSD). TUSD sits to the southwest of Sacramento and serves students from Fairfield, Vacaville, and Travis Air Force Base. Sharon Hutchins, who was president of TUSD Board of Education at the time of Fielder's consultancy, could not recall the specific impetus for the board's decision to hire Fielder, but said that Fielder conducted a school life study to help the board better understand and improve the K-12 school environment. [8]

At TUSD, Fielder created a program she titled, "Building a Community of Learners." Rather than designing a study to identify trends within the school environment, Fielder trained the districts' students, teachers, and administrators to develop and conduct their own studies. Under Fielder's guidance, district teachers created surveys which they administered to high school students. Following these interviews, high school students interviewed middle school students, and middle school students interviewed elementary school students. Hutchins recalled that Fielder's approach was rooted in cultural anthropology and was focused on building mutual interdependence for learning. Although Hutchins did not remember Fielder referring to a specific methodological framework, the methodology she used in "Building a Community of Learners" bears a striking resemblance to participatory action research. [9]

In addition to helping the district design and execute a school life study, Fielder's program was designed to facilitate bidirectional learning, which would help teachers become learners and students become teachers. By the time she began working with TUSD, Fielder had developed a philosophy that maintained that the core of any educational endeavor was the relationships between students and teachers. To build successful relationships, teachers and students needed to recognize their interdependence and cultivate respect and appreciation for each other. Staff, teachers, and administers also learned to become vulnerable and open in their interactions with students because in order for the school culture to shift, they had to model the culture in which they wanted the students to engage. As a result of Fielder's work, the school board began to view the district through the lens of becoming learners of their own environments.

Additionally, Fielder taught TUSD that schools could not isolate themselves from the complexities of the real world. Shortly before the district hired Fielder, a video surfaced of officers of the Los Angeles Police Department beating an African American man, Rodney King. Four officers were charged with using excessive force. Riots erupted across Los Angeles when a jury acquitted three of the officers and failed to reach a verdict in the case of the fourth officer. The riots lasted for six days, during which 63 people were killed and more than 2000 injured. The riots ended only after then-Governor Pete Wilson called on the National Guard to re-establish order (Matheson & Baade, 2004). Sharon Hutchins, who had been a part of TUSD's decision to hire Marie Fielder, did not believe that racial tensions resulting from the Rodney King case were the primary motivation for the hiring decision, but reverberations from the King case were felt throughout the United States and no doubt affected the students in TUSD.

For Hutchins, the success of Fielder's work in the district was not the specific findings of the school life study, but the process through which the district undertook the study. Moreover, throughout the school life study, Fielder championed the importance of learning from mistakes. Hutchins recalled that shortly after the study concluded and the data were analyzed, a staff member found a small box of surveys under a table. The data from those surveys had not been included in the data analysis. Some district members were tempted to use the unanalyzed data as a reason to undermine the validity of the study's findings, but Fielder turned it into a learning opportunity. When given the box of newly discovered surveys, Fielder put the box on a table and said, "This is great! What do we learn from our environment when we find things that have been misplaced?"

Hutchins said that learning how to respond and recover from failure was one of the greatest lessons that Marie Fielder taught. She recalled that Fielder celebrated the fact that she was once fired as a tremendous opportunity for learning. Hutchins remembered that Fielder was somewhat disappointed when she learned that Hutchins had never been fired. Fielder told her, "I hope one day you're fired and have an opportunity for that learning experience." Fielder was distinctively aware of the impact that failure can have on a person, including their ability to re-adjust after such failure without self-pity. Specifically, she believed people needed to move quickly to transform the experience into a celebration and learning opportunity.

According to Hutchins, Fielder was contemplating the curriculum for the doctoral program in Educational Leadership for Change while she was consulting with TUSD. By that time, Hutchins and Fielder had become friends, and Fielder invited Hutchins to her home, where they sat at Fielder's kitchen table, where she did most of her work, and brainstormed ideas for the curriculum. Fielder's ideas for the curriculum centered around the need for reflective learning and practice. She believed that the absence of reflection impedes growth or development. The importance of reflective practice remains a tenant of Fielding's doctoral program. As Hutchins recalled their friendship, she said, "Marie was dynamic — always introducing new ideas and new methodologies. She was a trailblazer to the very end."

Marie Fielder while teaching at San Francisco State College
(*Courtesy, Nicola Smith*).

# Chapter 4

# Mentoring the Next Generation

*Fielding Graduate University and the School of Educational Leadership for Change*

Marie Fielder's role in the founding of Fielding Graduate University is acknowledged in the institution's history, but the true impact she had on the development of the university has not been fully explored. Fielding was founded in 1974 by Frederic Hudson, Hallock Hoffman, and Renate Tesch to serve mid-career adults whose education needs were not being met by traditional universities (Melville, 2016). Fielding offers graduate degrees in education, psychology, and human and organizational development via a distributed learning model that combines elements of in-person and distance learning. As a member of the founding Board of Trustees, Fielder played a key role in the organization's founding, and she later served as a faculty member in the university's doctoral program in Educational Leadership for Change. Keith Melville has written an authoritative history of Fielding's founding and development. This chapter does not offer a revision to that history. Rather, it expands the knowledge of Fielder's contributions to the university as they were remembered by her students, colleagues, and daughter, Nicola Smith.

Marie Fielder met Hallock Hoffman when they worked together at the Pacifica Foundation in the 1960s, and it was Hoffman who invited her to serve on Fielding's first board. Fielder agreed, in part because she believed that movements for progressive social change need to be embodied in organizations that would help carry such movements forward. Fielder thought the new university, which was then comprised of only a few faculty and prospective students, had the potential to be such an organization (Melville, 2016). Fielder quickly became an influential member of the board. According to Fielder's daughter, Nicola Smith, the board of a nascent organization plays as important a role in its founding as the organization's executive officers, and Fielding's first board played a central role in establishing the organization's mission, values, and policies that made the university unique. For example, it was members of Fielding's first board who secured well-known scholar of adult learning Malcolm Knowles as a faculty member.

The university's name, Fielding, bears lasting testimony to Fielder's influence. Anna DiStefano, who joined Fielding in 1983 as an assistant program director and later served as Fielding's provost, recalled the version of the origins of Fielding's name she learned while moderating a discussion of Fielding's founding during the university's 25th anniversary celebration. DiStefano said she had previously heard that the name Fielding was combination of the last names of Marie Fielder and Bob Goulding. Fielder had been one of Hoffman's mentors, and Goulding, who was head of the Western Institute for Group and Family Therapy and enthusiastic about the potential of a new university that would provide clinical training in transactional analysis, was one of Hudson's mentors

(Melville, 2016). After combining Fielder and Goulding into the name Fielding, Hudson and Hoffman asked people they met on the streets of Los Angeles and San Francisco what they thought about the work of the Fielding Institute. The responses they received were positive, and the people they spoke with thought Fielding was an impressive place, even though the institution was not yet in existence. However, when DiStefano asked Hoffman if the story was true, he said it was not. Hoffman told DiStefano that initially he wanted to name the organization The Redfield Institute, after Robert Redfield, a professor he had studied with during his undergraduate education. However, when Hoffman and Hudson surveyed people about their impressions of the Redfield Institute, the responses they received suggested that the name Redfield conjured up images of a little red schoolhouse, so they decided upon the name Fielding. DiStefano apparently had some doubts about the veracity of that version of events, and she continues to consider the name Fielding an homage to Fielder and Goulding.

Nicola Smith also believes that the name Fielding was a combination of Fielder and Goulding, and she points to the large portraits of the two that hung in Fielding's original offices. Toward the end of his life, Goulding told her mother, "Marie, you make sure Fielding remembers us. We mama-ed and papa-ed that organization into existence." Perhaps in honor of Goulding's request, Smith shared with me a piece of Fielding lore she does not believe is widely known. On Fielder's 57th birthday, March 11, 1974, Fielding's articles of incorporation were signed in her Berkeley home.

Fielder was still a member of the board when Anna DiStefano joined Fielding in 1983. Anna recalled that the university was thrown into a state of flux shortly thereafter. In 1985, Fielding received its first formal accreditation by the Western Association of Schools and Colleges (WASC). WASC informed the university that it would not need to seek reaccreditation for several years, and DiStefano said that WASC's departure "let the internal forces of conflict loose." Frederic Hudson had one specific vision for Fielding's direction, and Hallock Hoffman had another, very different vision. The tension between the two founders grew and began to spill over into the board, which was composed of friends and collogues of Hudson and Hoffman. The board could have easily fallen apart. Rather than capitulate to internal conflicts, the board, of which Fielder was a part, negotiated the retirements of all the founders as a way of preserving the institution. Distefano said, "I think Marie could have just as easily resigned from the board, and said, 'you figure it out,' but she and the rest of the Board were invested in Fielding and its continuation."

When Don MacIntyre became Fielding's third president in the early 1990s, he envisioned an additional doctoral program, which would offer both a clear benefit societal benefit and provide another source of revenue for the university. DiStefano accepted a two-year appointment as vice president of planning and program development to identify opportunities for new programming. In 1996, she helped start the Educational Leadership for Change doctoral program. MacIntyre lived in the Bay Area prior to his appointment as Fielding's president, and he knew Marie Fielder was an influential figure in public education. Having served as a board member for many years, Fielder became an external advisor, helping Fielding develop its new program.

## Chapter 4: Mentoring the Next Generation

As her tenure as vice president ended, DiStefano transitioned into the newly created role of Provost, and she oversaw the Educational Leadership for Change program. DiStefano traveled to Fielder's home in the Berkeley Hills, initially to solicit a donation for the new program. DiStefano recalled, "Marie never said, no. She just redirected you." Their meeting drew to a close with Fielder telling DiStefano that her daughter, Nicola, would be in touch with her. Smith later approached DiStefano, and said quite plainly, "What you should know is that my mother wants a job." DiStefano was surprised. It had not occurred to her that Marie Fielder would be interested in serving as a faculty member. In fact, DiStefano remembered thinking that Fielder was so accomplished that she would be above accepting a faculty position, but that was not how Fielder felt about the situation. Marie Fielder became an early faculty member of the Educational Leadership for Change program, and immediately attracted many students who knew of her reputation. Fielder remained a member of Fielding's faculty until she passed in 2002.

Judy Kuipers, who served as Fielding's president from 2000 through 2009, imagined that Fielder was not thrilled when she was appointed president because she had come from a traditional academic background, having served as chancellor at the University of Wisconsin prior to joining Fielding. Kuipers recalled that Fielder was a faculty member, not a board member, during her tenure as president, but Fielder willingly served as a consultant whenever Kuipers needed advice. Early in her presidency, Kuipers went to Fielder with a struggle she was having. Fielder's response was brief but caring, and her advice helped put Kuipers back on track. Kuipers never saw Fielder lose her temper but said that she would let you know if she thought you were heading in the wrong direction because she was very values oriented. Kuipers recalled, "Marie was a mentor to me and taught me the importance of serving as a mentor toward others." As evidence of the lasting impact of Fielder's emphasis on mentorship, Kuipers, who is now retired, currently serves as a mentor to the executive leadership at Fresno State University.

Virgine Thomas-Cotter was mentored by Marie Fielder. Thomas-Cotter enrolled in Fielding's doctoral program in Education, Leadership, and Change after she was offered the opportunity to serve as dean of a school of the arts but needed to earn a doctoral degree in order to fully qualify for the position. She first met Fielder during an orientation session in Atlanta. Fielder was fascinated when Thomas-Cotter introduced herself as teacher at a school of animation, and Thomas-Cotter arranged for Fielder to have a tour of an animation school affiliated with the institute where she taught later that afternoon. As the two women chatted in the cab ride back to the orientation session, she asked Fielder to serve as her faculty mentor. Fielder replied, "I thought you'd never ask!"

Thomas-Cotter recalled that Fielder was a self-effacing person who never talked much about accomplishments. She learned of Fielder's work in civil rights only after she graduated from Fielding. Thomas-Cotter was determined to complete her doctoral program in 18 months, and Fielder supported her in this pursuit. After she graduated, she learned that Fielding's administration was unhappy with her ability to complete her doctoral program so quickly, and they created a policy requiring a minimum time period that students needed to be enrolled in the university before they could graduate.

In some respects, Thomas-Cotter's ability to graduate in 18 months paid homage to the unique approach Fielding's founders took to adult education. As Nicola Smith recalled, the founders were "iconoclasts. They did things their own way."

Marie Fielder with her mother, Ellee Fielder and her daughter Nicola Smith in Boston, ca. 1970 (*Courtesy, Nicola Smith*).

# Epilogue

# The Legacy of Marie Fielder

When Orlando Taylor joined Fielding Graduate University in 2014 as the vice president for strategic initiatives and research, he immediately noticed the absence of people of color from accounts of the University's history. After speaking with Nicola Smith, who currently serves as a faculty member in Fielding's School of Leadership Studies, and learning of her mother's role in the founding of Fielding, he decided to establish the Marie Fielder Center for Democracy, Leadership, and Education. The interdisciplinary center, which opened in 2015, promotes research that advances the cause of social justice, and it encourages collaboration among all of Fielding's programs. During their remarks following the dedication of the Marie Fielder Center, Taylor and Fielding's current president, Katrina Rogers, said, "Through the Marie Fielder Center, Fielding reaffirms its commitment to conduct the research, provide the public and academic education, and engage in the advocacy of diverse communities" (Melville, 2016, p. 55). The annual awarding of the Marie Fielder Medal for Social Transformation is among of the center's current initiatives. Past recipients include Walter Bumphus, president and CEO of the American Association of Community Colleges; Gary Orfield, a noted civil rights scholar; Patricia Gurin, professor emerita of psychology and women's studies at the University of Michigan; Dolores Huerta, labor leader and co-founder of the National Farmworkers Association, and Angela Davis, legendary scholar and civil rights activist. The Marie Fielder Center also offers graduate fellowships to Fielding students engaged in research and advocacy that aligns with the center's mission.

The center's relevance to the ongoing pursuit of social justice was made clear when George Floyd was murdered by a Minneapolis police officer on May 25, 2020. Floyd's murder sparked renewed protests against police brutality, and mass demonstrations in support of the Black Lives Matter movement were held across the country. On June 3, 2020, Orlando Taylor wrote a memo to the members of the Fielder Center Advisory Council and Fielder Graduate Fellows, calling for the center's recommitment to Marie Fielder's legacy and the cause of racial justice. He wrote, "We dishonor Marie Fielder and others who we have recognized for paying the price for advocating and advancing social justice beyond mere words and slogans by remaining silent or intellectualizing on issues of blatant racism and exclusion that are staring us in the face – just as they have for centuries" (O. Taylor, personal communication).

Throughout my work on this project, I have had many opportunities to consider Taylor's call for renewed commitment to racial equity, and I have often wondered how Marie Fielder may have responded to the current manifestations of institutionalized racial violence in the United States. Many of the people I interviewed in the course of my research shared their thoughts on this question. Sharon Hutchins suggested that Fielder would focus on bidirectional learning. She said,

"I don't know that Marie would view the struggles of

today as any different from the struggles of yesterday. The challenge is the same, but how we very the challenge has changed. The trailblazers of the 1950s and 1960s would have a lot to teach, but Marie would also want them to learn from the new generation."

Mark Scanlon-Greene echoed Hutchins' sentiments, noting that Fielder would likely see the contemporary struggle for racial justice as an opportunity to leverage change. He observed that there are currently many grassroots and community movements trying to bring about change including those attempting to replace conservative prosecutors with progressive prosecutors. Scanlon-Greene believed that Fielder would be working to help those prosecutors get elected. Beverly Palley suggested that Fielder would step back to consider how the United States had arrived at a moment where Black Lives Matter would be a slogan needing to be uttered, and she would champion efforts to require comprehensive education in the field of Black and Ethnic Studies.

In May 2022, I participated in a panel on leadership in high education at a virtual conference convened by Fielding Graduate University. During my remarks, I highlighted the importance Fielder placed on intergroup dialogue designed to engage people across political difference. After the panel concluded, I worried that I had inadvertently suggested that racism and other forms of oppression should be welcomed in public discourse. Nothing could be further from the truth. Fielder believed that racism was anathema, but the people who espoused racist beliefs should be treated with the dignity to which we are all entitled. It is only by recognizing our shared humanity that we can heal the racial scars that have been etched into the fabric of American society. This is a lesson Marie Fielder taught me as I studied her life, and it is but one of the lasting legacies she has bequeathed to us.

# ENDNOTES

A note on sources: Most of the information contained in this monograph is taken from primary sources. Fielder's daughter, Nicola Smith, and I conducted 10 oral history interviews with people who knew Marie Fielder. Nicola also provided me with several hundred pages of her mother's papers, which included resumes, professional reports, newspaper clippings, calendars, and personal correspondence. The most significant piece of archival material was contained in Fielder's nomination for the 1999 Women of Achievement Vision and Excellence (WAVE) Award, which contained extensive biographical information, along with documentation of many of Fielder's professional accomplishments. Additional archival material was provided by Lenneal Henderson, Anna DiStefano, and Margo Okazawa-Rey. Although extremely useful, the archival material was also limited in that newspaper clippings and magazine articles often did not contain the name of the publication or the year in which the article was published. When citing these sources, I reference all available information with the acknowledgement that it is incomplete.

[1] Marie Fielder interview with Ernest Rosenbaum, M.D. The interview was conducted in 2001 while Dr. Fielder was undergoing chemotherapy and was not broadcast. The VHS tape is in Nicola Smith's personal collection. Subsequent references to this interview are cited Rosenbaum, 2001.

[2] Unless otherwise noted, the information contained in this monograph, including direct quotes attributed to Fielder, are taken from the interviews conducted for this project.

[3] Nicola Smith recalled the names of these two professors but could not recall the first name of Dr. Bloomberg.

[4] Desegregation refers to the placing of interracial groups in the same physical environment, while integration refers to the social processes through which interracial groups interact within a given environment. Although technically different, desegregation and integration are complementary processes, and because Fielder worked to promote both, I use the terms interchangeably (See Krovetz, 1972).

[5] While writing this chapter, I was fortunate to stumble across Favors' (1969) dissertation on the Berkeley Intergroup Education Project run by Marie Fielder. My understanding of Fielder's work with BUSD is largely due to Favor's research.

[6] The information regarding Fielder's work with RUSD is taken from a 300-page report she submitted to The Department of Health Education and Welfare, Office of Education.

[7] Unlike traditional research methodologies in which the researcher serves an expert who identifies and explains the primary issues in a study, a researcher using participatory action research will ask a community to define the issues they are interested in understanding and then help community members learn to collect and analyze the data they find most relevant to the issue they are researching (Sprague, 2005).

# REFERENCES

Anderson, K. (2004). The Little Rock school desegregation crisis: Moderation and social conflict. *The Journal of Southern History, 70*(3), 603–36. https://doi.org/10.2307/27648479.

Behnken, B.P. (2012). *The struggle in black and brown: African American and Mexican American relations during the civil rights era.* University of Nebraska Press.

Berry, L. (1967). Report on the student participation in the Richmond training center. *Leadership training institute in problems of school desegregation.* (M. Fielder & L. Dyckman, Eds.). Office of Education (DHEW).

Brodo, L. (1999). The age of work. *Working Woman.*

Chavez, L. & Frankenberg, E. (2009). *Integration defended: Berkeley Unified's strategy to maintain diversity.* UC Berkeley Berkeley Law School Warren Institute on Race, Ethnicity & Diversity and UCLA Civil Rights Project.

Cluster, D. (1979). Mass movements made the decade: An introduction." *They should have served that cup of coffee: 7 radicals remember the 60s* (D. Cluster, ed.). South End Press, xi-xvi.

Dittmer, J. (1995). *Local people: The struggle for civil rights in Mississippi.* University of Illinois Press.

Favors, K.T. (1969). *A Study of the Intergroup Education Project of the Berkeley Unified School District.* (Publication No. 6918868). [Doctoral Dissertation: University of California, Berkeley]. ProQuest Dissertation Publishing.

Fielder, M. & Dyckman, L. (1967). *Leadership training institute in problems of school desegregation.* Office of Education (DHEW).

Getzels, J.W. & Jackson, P.W. (1962). *Creativity and intelligence: Explorations with gifted students.* Wiley.

Green. K. (2015). *Something must be done about Prince*

Edward County: A family, a Virginia town, a civil rights battle*. Harper Publishing.

Grier, W.H. & Cobbs, P.M. (1968) *Black rage*. Basic Books.

Hillis, M.R. (1995). Allison Davis and the study of race, social calls, and schooling. *Journal of Negro Education*, 64(1), 33-41.

Holding, R. (2002). Marie Fielder – pioneering educator / Berkeley woman had long list of firsts. *San Francisco Chronicle*. https://www.sfgate.com/bayarea/article/Marie-Fielder-pioneering-educator-Berkeley-2826870.php

Kirp, D.L., Fine, D., & Angelides (1979). Desegregations, politics, and the courts: Race and schooling policy in Richmond, California. *American Journal of Education, 88* (1), 32-82.

Krovetz, M. L. (1972). Desegregation or integration: Which is our goal? *The Phi Delta Kappan, 54*(4), 247–249.

Manning, M.L. (2010). Havighurst's development tasks, young adolescents and diversity." *The Clearing House: A Journal of Educational, Strategies, and Ideas*, 2, 75-78.

McNeill, W.H. (1991). *Hutchins' university: A memoir of the University of Chicago, 1929-1950*. University of Chicago Press.

McVeigh, Rory. "Structural Incentives for Conservative Mobilization: Power Devaluation and the Rise of the Ku Klux Klan, 1915-1925." *Social Forces* 77, (1999): 1461-1496.

Melville, K. (2016). *A passion for adult learning: How the Fielding model is transforming doctoral education*. Fielding University Press.

Mercer, J. (1968). *A manual for the evaluation desegregation in California public schools. Section 1: Schema for Describing the Desegregation Process in Public School Districts of California*. Riverside Unified School District. California State Department of Education.

Motley, W. (1989). *Knock on any door*. Northern Illinois

# References

University Press. (Original work published 1947)

Mude, W., Oguoma, V.M., Nyanhanda, T., Mwanri, L., and Njue, C. (2021). "Racial disparities in COVID-19 pandemic cases, hospitalisations, and deaths: A systematic review and meta-analysis." *Journal of Global Health 11.*

National Aeronautical and Space Administration. (2011). *NASA headquarters oral history project: Harriet Jenkins.* https://historycollection.jsc.nasa.gov/JSCHistoryPortal/history/oral_histories/NASA_HQ/Administrators/JenkinsHG/jenkinshg.htm

Noguera, P.A. Ties that bind, forces that divide: Berkeley high school and the challenge of integration." *USFL Rev.* 29 (1994): 719.

Reed, R.J. (1982). School boards, the community, and school desegregation. *Journal of Black Studies, 13*(2), 189-206.

Spinnet, Laura. *Pale Rider: The Spanish Flu of 1918 and How It Changed the World.* PublicAffairs.

Sprague, J. (2005). *Feminist methodologies for critical researchers: Bridging differences.* Altamira Press.

Wilson, A.B. (1967). Problems in race relations in Richmond. *Leadership training institute in problems of school desegregation.* (M. Fielder & L. Dyckman, Eds.). Office of Education (DHEW).

## About the Author

Jenny Johnson-Riley, PhD is a scholar-activist working at the intersections of race and gender in the movement to end violence against women. She earned her PhD in Human Development from Fielding Graduate University, where she also held the honor of serving as a member of the inaugural cohort of doctoral fellows at the Marie Fielding Center from Democracy, Leadership, and Education. Jenny Johnson-Riley has presented her research at the National Conference on Race and Ethnicity in Higher Education and National Women's Studies Association.

Jenny Johnson-Riley's professional work includes counseling survivors and perpetrators of sexual violence, program development, and public policy consulting. She currently works in a private psychotherapy practice in Washington state and is on the Board of Directors for the Washington State Association for the Treatment and Prevention of Sexual Abuse.